THIS WALKER BOOK BELONGS TO:

_____

_____

_____

With thanks to Jean Millar,
numeracy consultant for BEAM (Be A Mathematician),
for her help during the preparation of this book.

First published 2002 by Walker Books Ltd
87 Vauxhall Walk, London SE11 5HJ

This edition published 2003

2 4 6 8 10 9 7 5 3

© 2002 Jessica Spanyol

This book has been typeset in Garamond Book Educational and Spanyol Bold

Printed in China

British Library Cataloguing in Publication Data: a catalogue record
for this book is available from the British Library.

ISBN 978-0-7445-9491-1

www.walkerbooks.co.uk

Carlo Likes Counting

Jessica Spanyol

3 goldfish

WALKER BOOKS
AND SUBSIDIARIES
LONDON • BOSTON • SYDNEY • AUCKLAND

Carlo and Mum count one.

2 bananas

2 apples

2 caps

3 ribbons

Carlo counts three in the park.

3 squirrels

3 sticks

3 roses

3
sisters

3 bags

Carlo and Crackers count four.

4 leaves

4 sacks

4 pipes

4 hatpins

4 feathers

4 cones

Carlo counts five
in the café.

5 cups

5 hot-dogs

5 bottles

5 peas

Carlo counts six over the stream.

6 baby birds

6 spots

6 flowers

6 stones

6 windows

6 fishes

Carlo and Dad count seven.

7 Bobbing Boats

Study with 7 Flowers

White Rabbits No.7

Still Life with 7 Oranges

7-House Town

Basket with 7 Kittens

7 red buckets

Carlo counts eight in the toyshop.

8 mice

8 legs

8 balls

9 feathers

Carlo counts nine
at the farm.

9 piglets

9 raindrops

9 patches

9 whiskers

9 chicks

Carlo likes
counting
very much.

And he loves splashing!

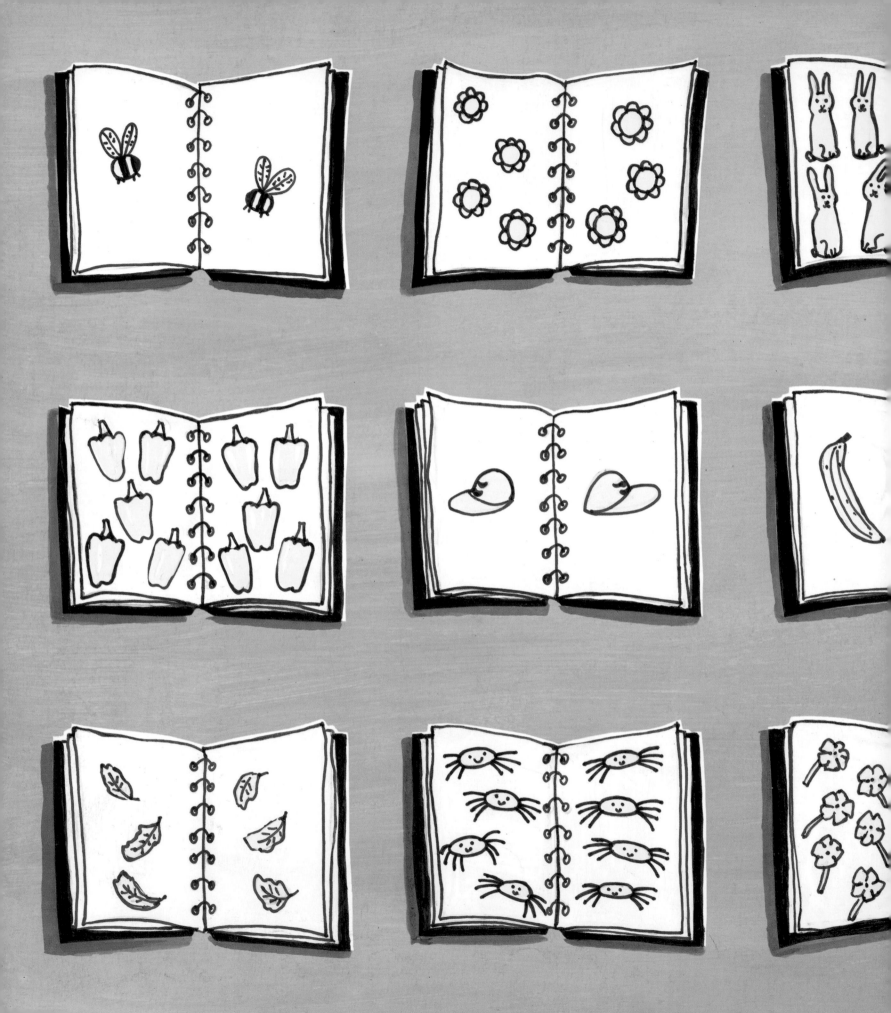